Relaxing Hawaiian Scenes III:
An Adult Coloring Book

by

Stephen Jorgensen
(artist)

published by
CyberSuccess Publishing
Honolulu, Hawaii

This book is a coloring book for adults. It is more complicated than a child's coloring book with smaller and finer details. You have to concentrate to color in all the small shapes. That makes it an ideal method to clear your mind of many negative thoughts and it helps you relieve stress. Coloring will reduce anxiety, and help you focus and will bring you more mindfulness. It is therapeutic.

This volume is the second in a series, it has more of the same kind of lovely Hawaiian flowers, fish and scenes as volume one.

This coloring book will bring the more of the beauty of Hawaii into your life. The next best thing to actually going there. All the work here is by the Hawaiian artist Stephen E Jorgensen. He has over 200 other works of beautiful Hawaiian art available on his Etsy website. Most of his work is large canvas wall hangings, some of which are reduced to coloring pages in this book. See these at hawaiiseascapes.etsy.com

ISBN-13: 978-1546550686

ISBN-10: 1546550682

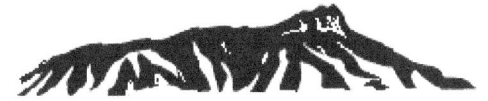

Relaxing Hawaiian Scenes III:
An Adult Coloring Book

Most of the pictures will require shading of the petal colors and perhaps the other colors to look nice. You can look at the full color reproductions shown on the front and the back covers to see what the shading could look like. You don't have to use the exact same colors for the images, try different colors. This coloring book doesn't have all the individual colors outlined by colors like my first two books, There is more room for the colorist to do their own shading.

Still many of the colors are just slightly different, so it is best to used a large selection of colored pencils to be able to find an appropriate color, and it helps to "layer" two different colors to get a better match. For instance, coloring a purple over a red will give a darker more scarlet red.

All the coloring pages are one side only, so no bleed-through will mess up a drawing on the opposite side of the page if you do use color marking pens.

Enjoy your coloring.

This Hawaiian Coloring Therapy
Will relax you.

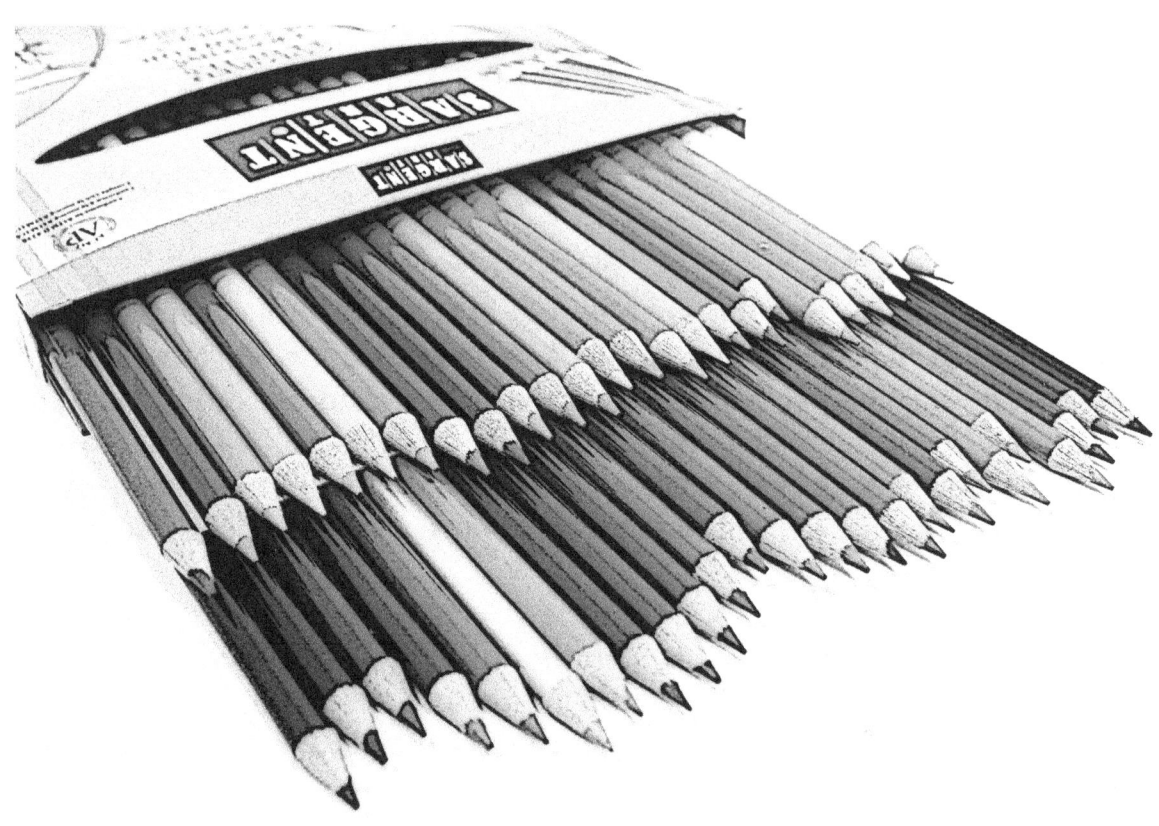

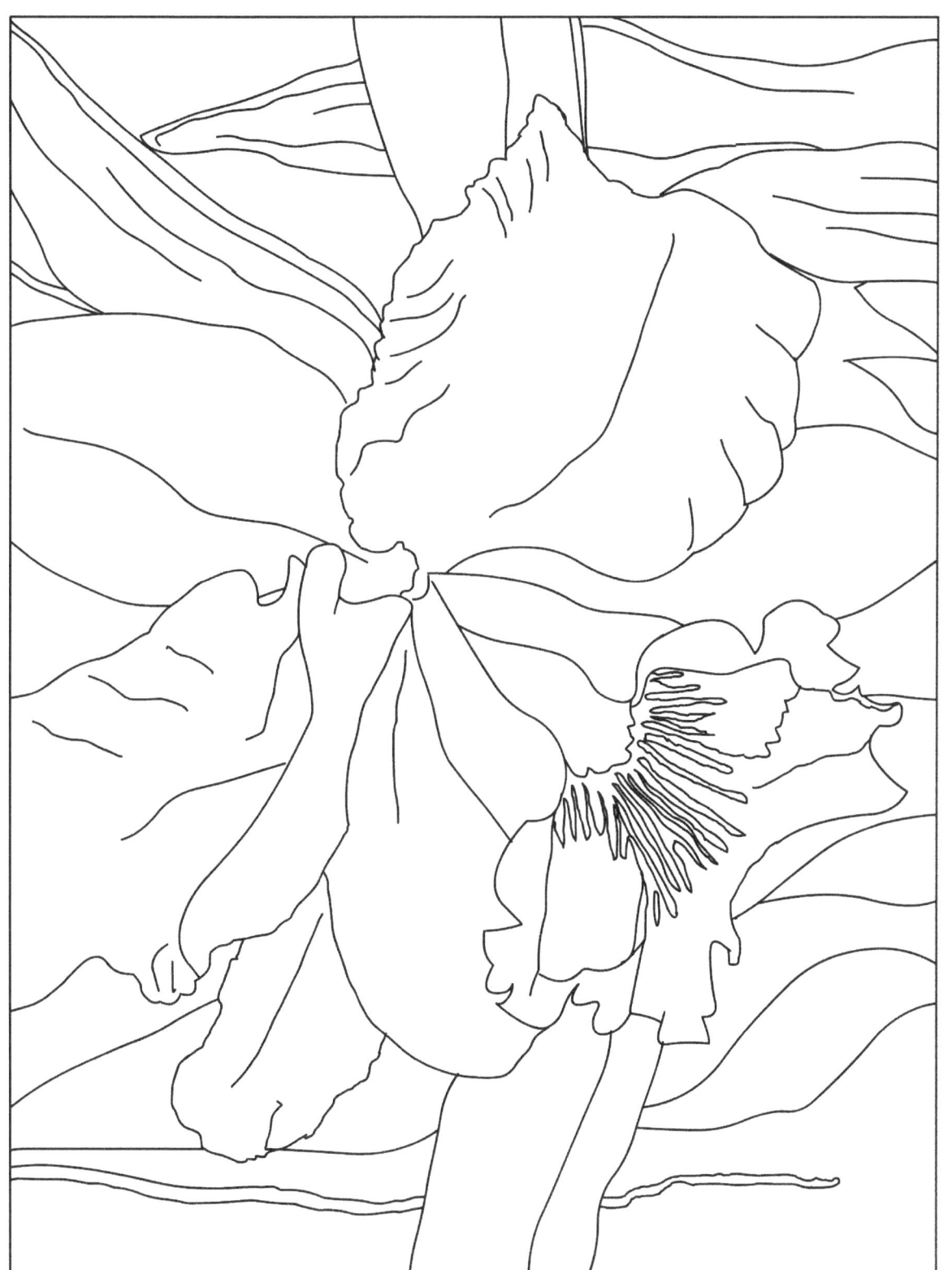

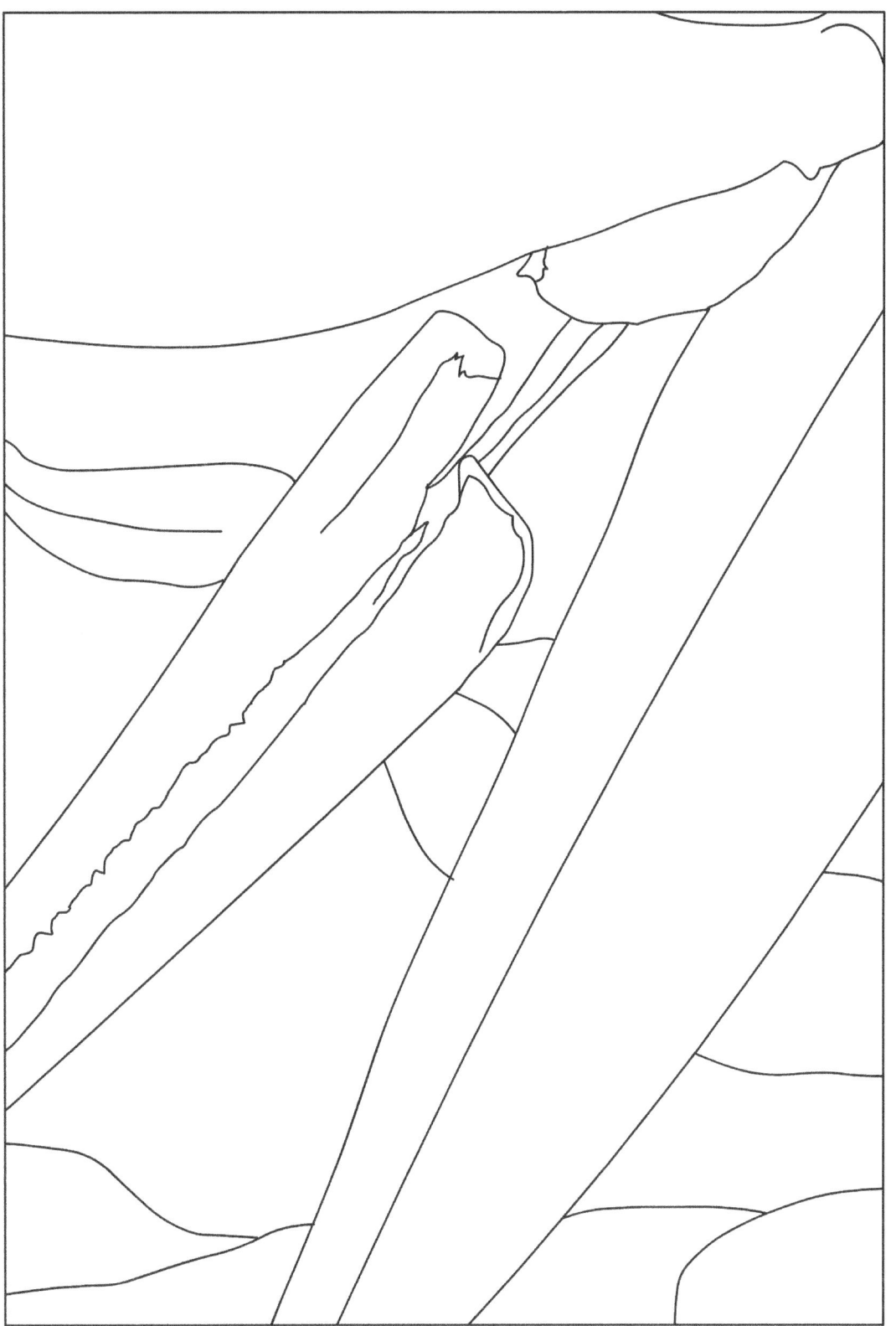

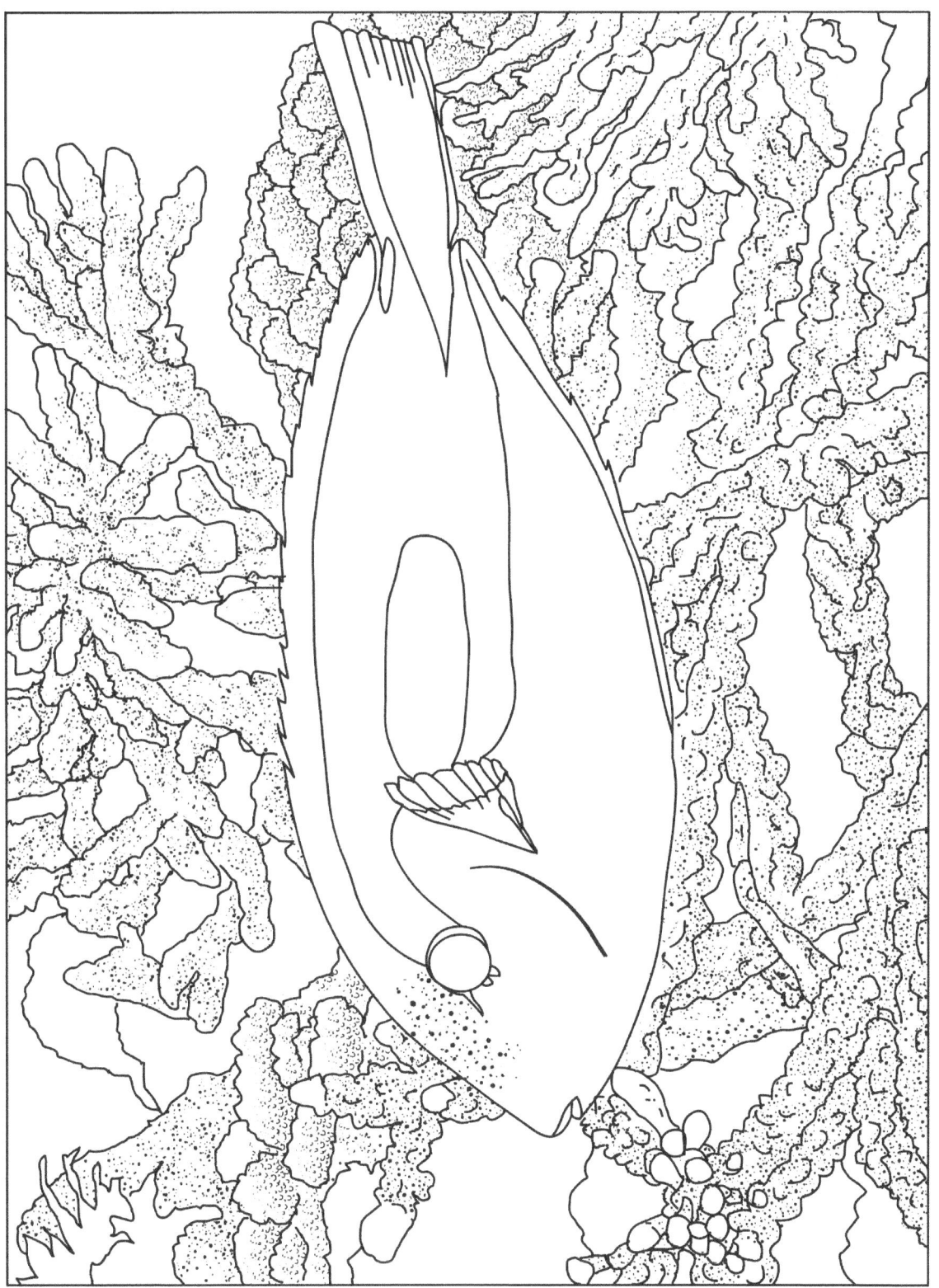

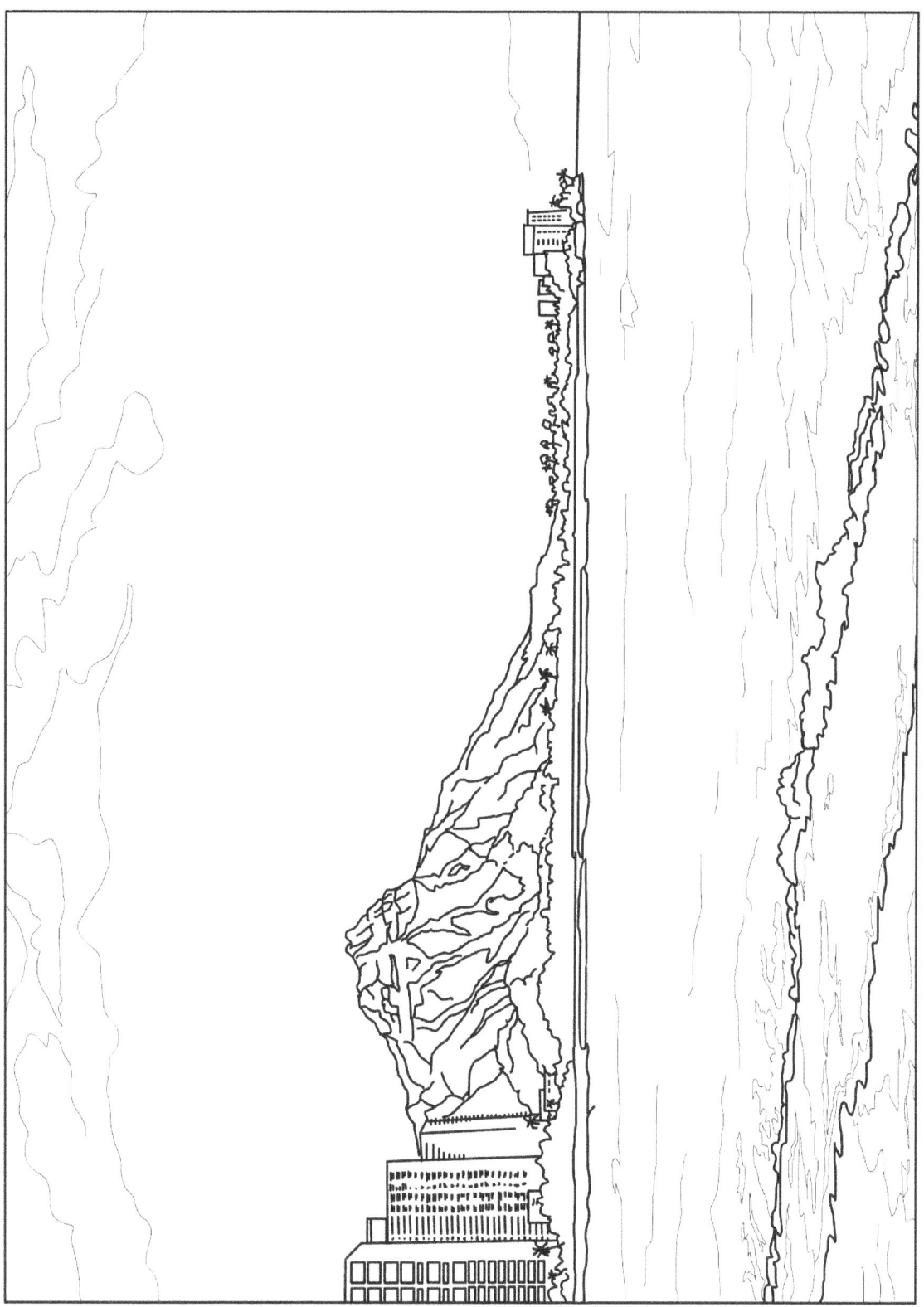

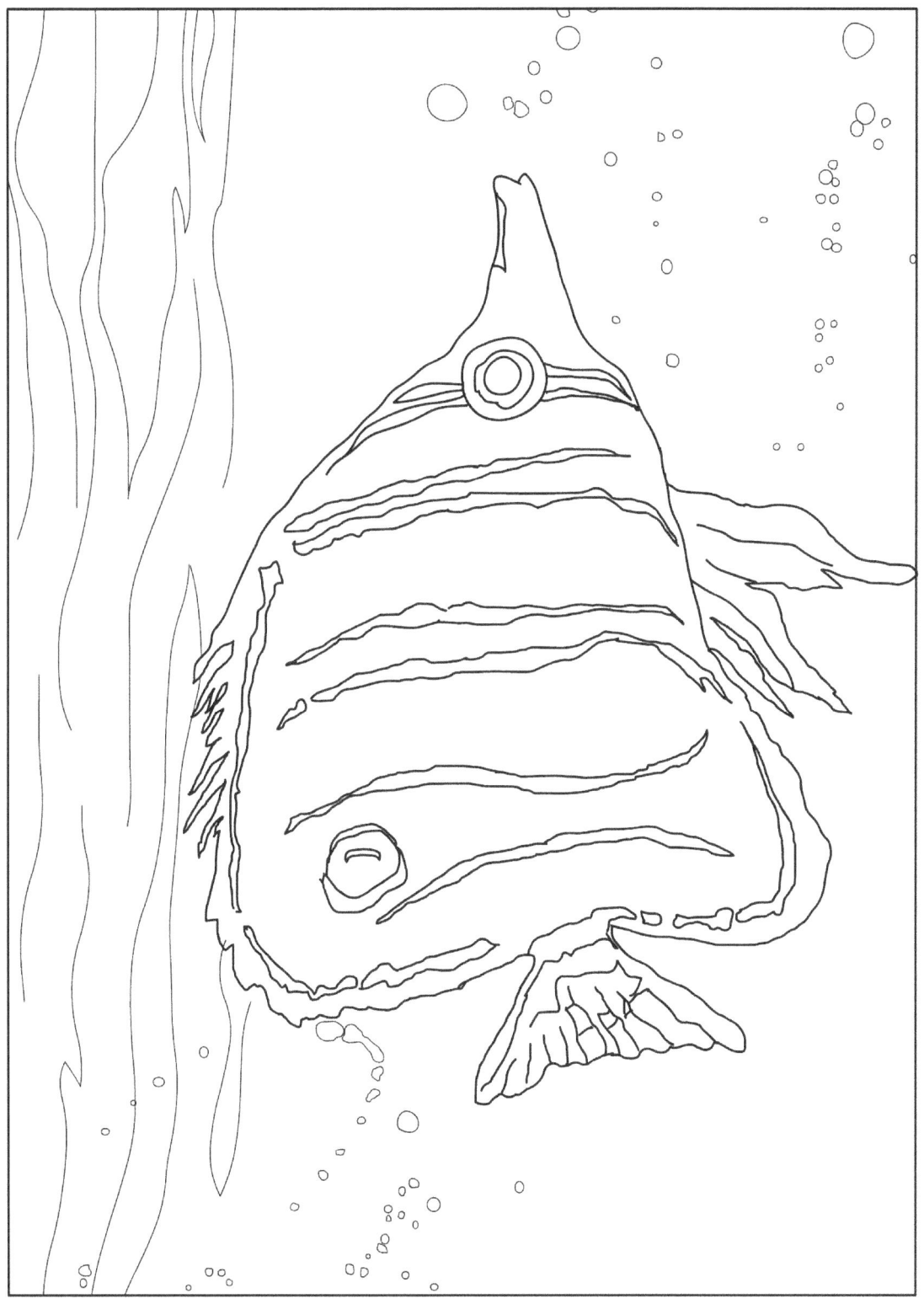

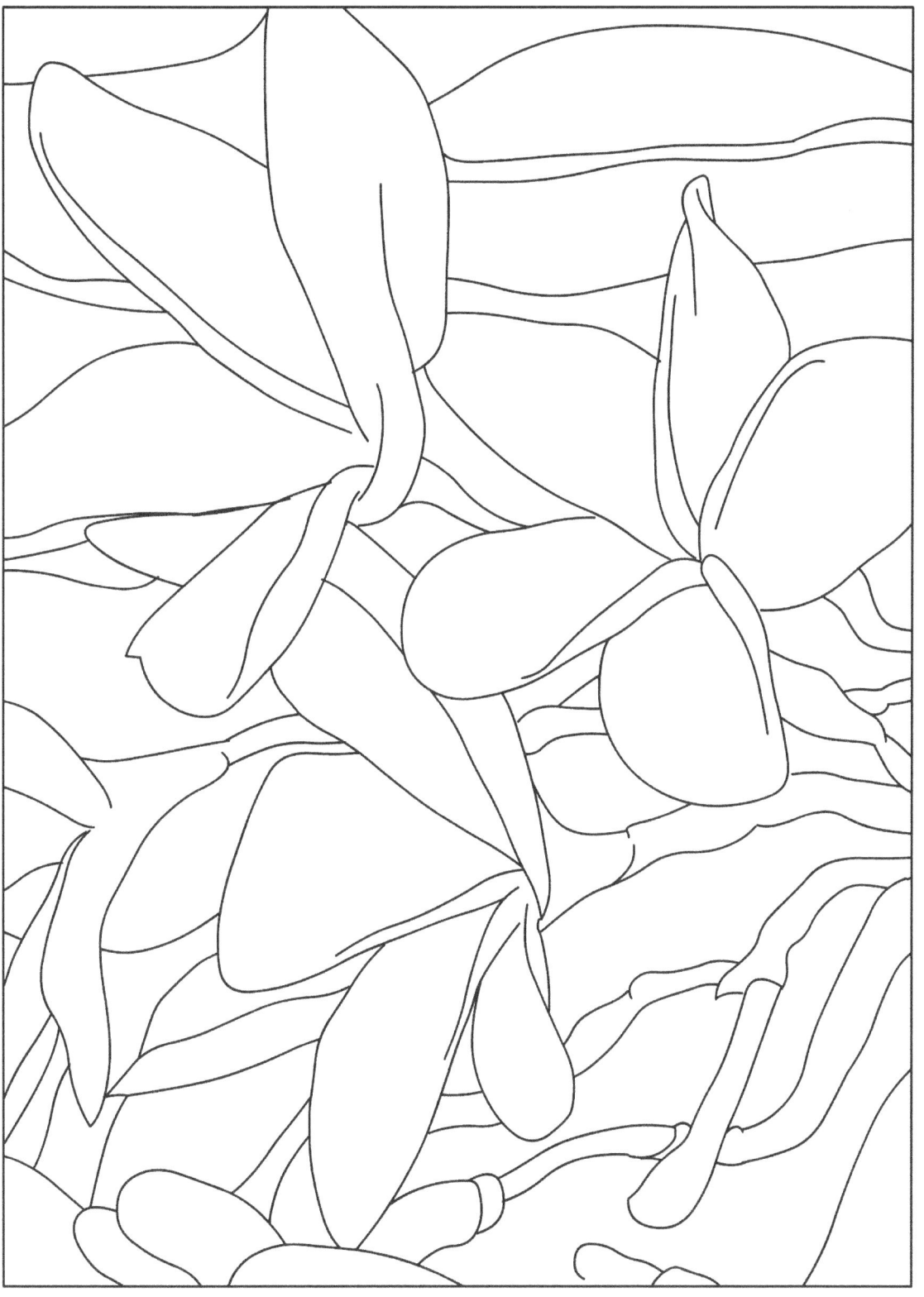

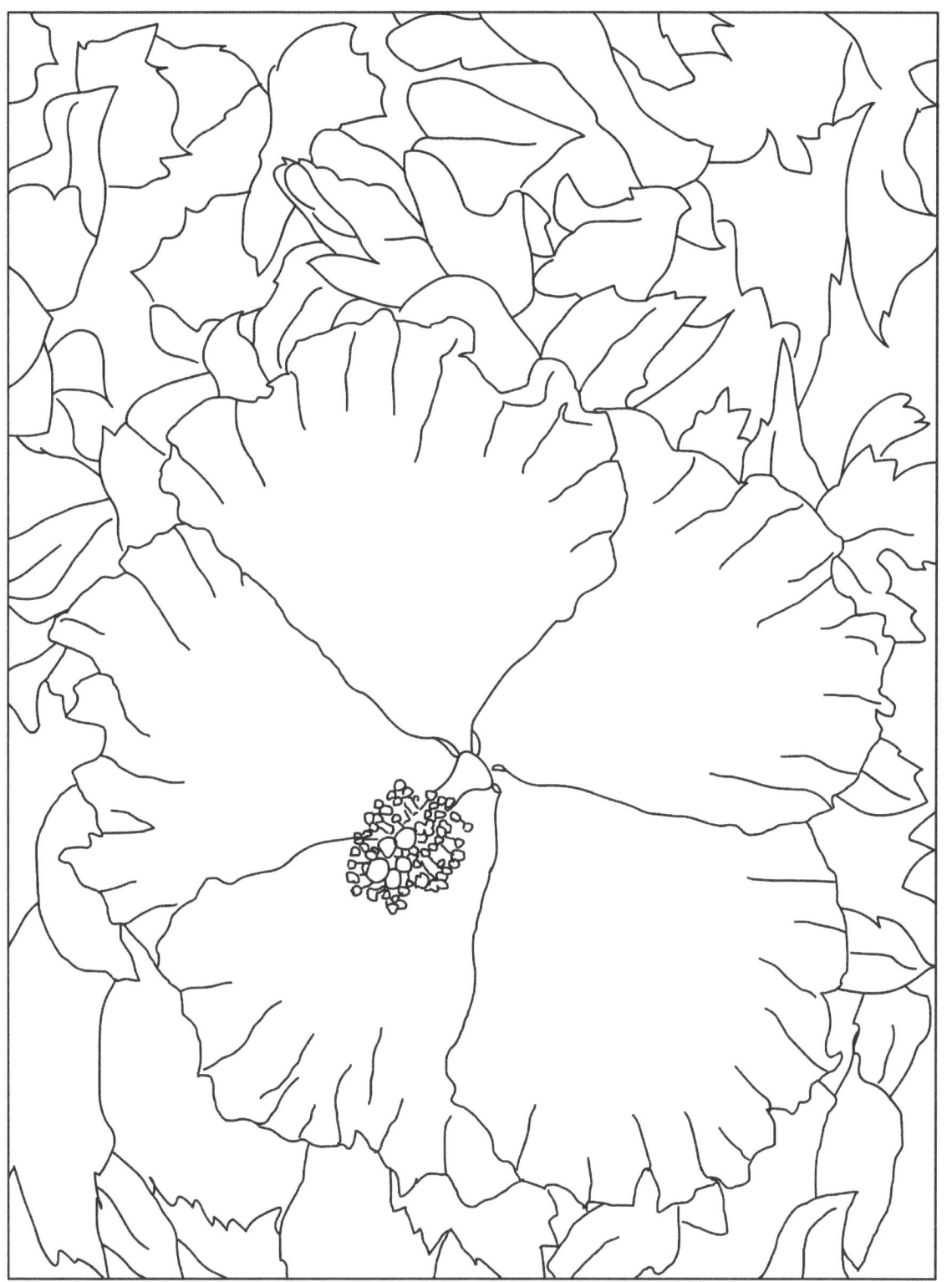

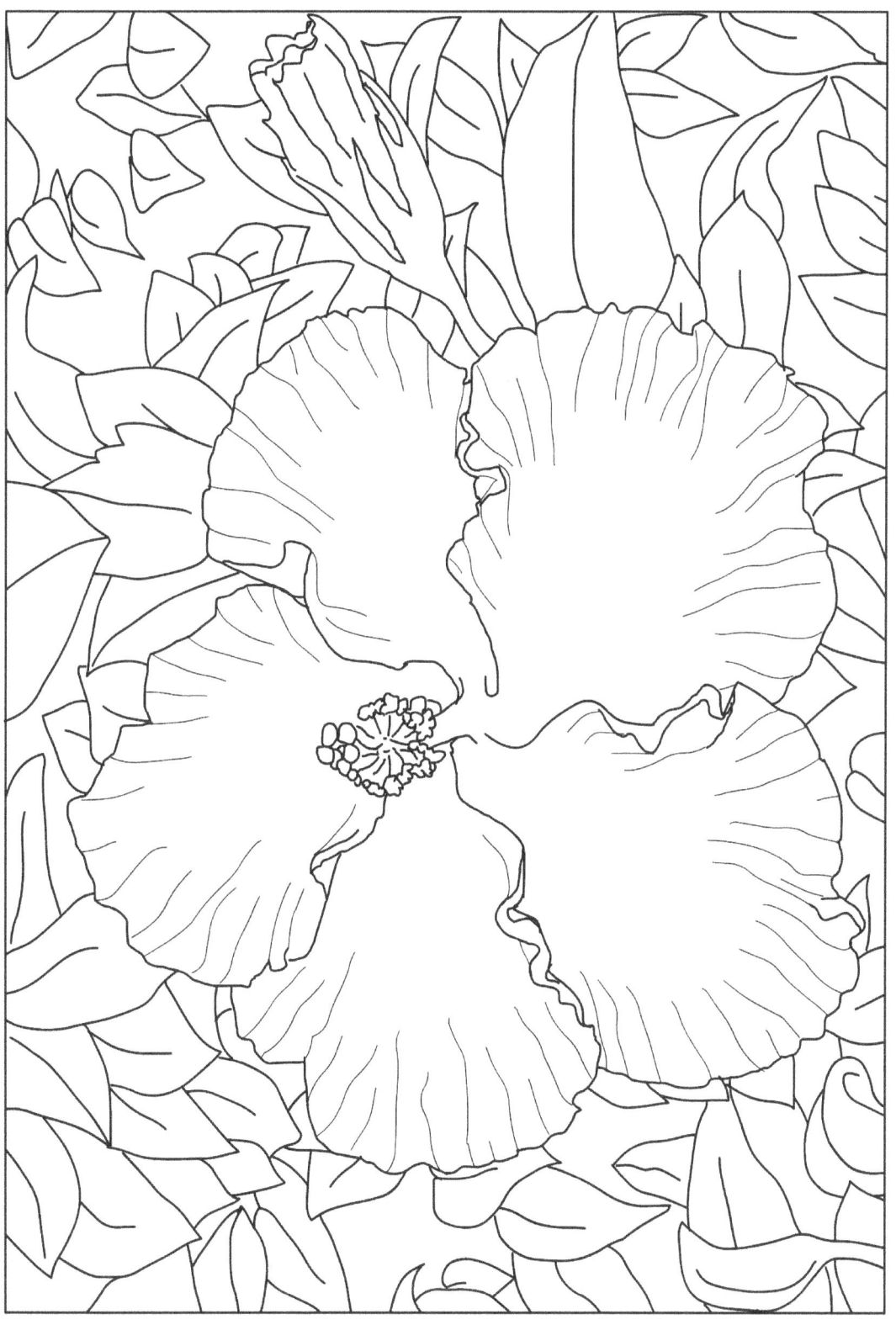

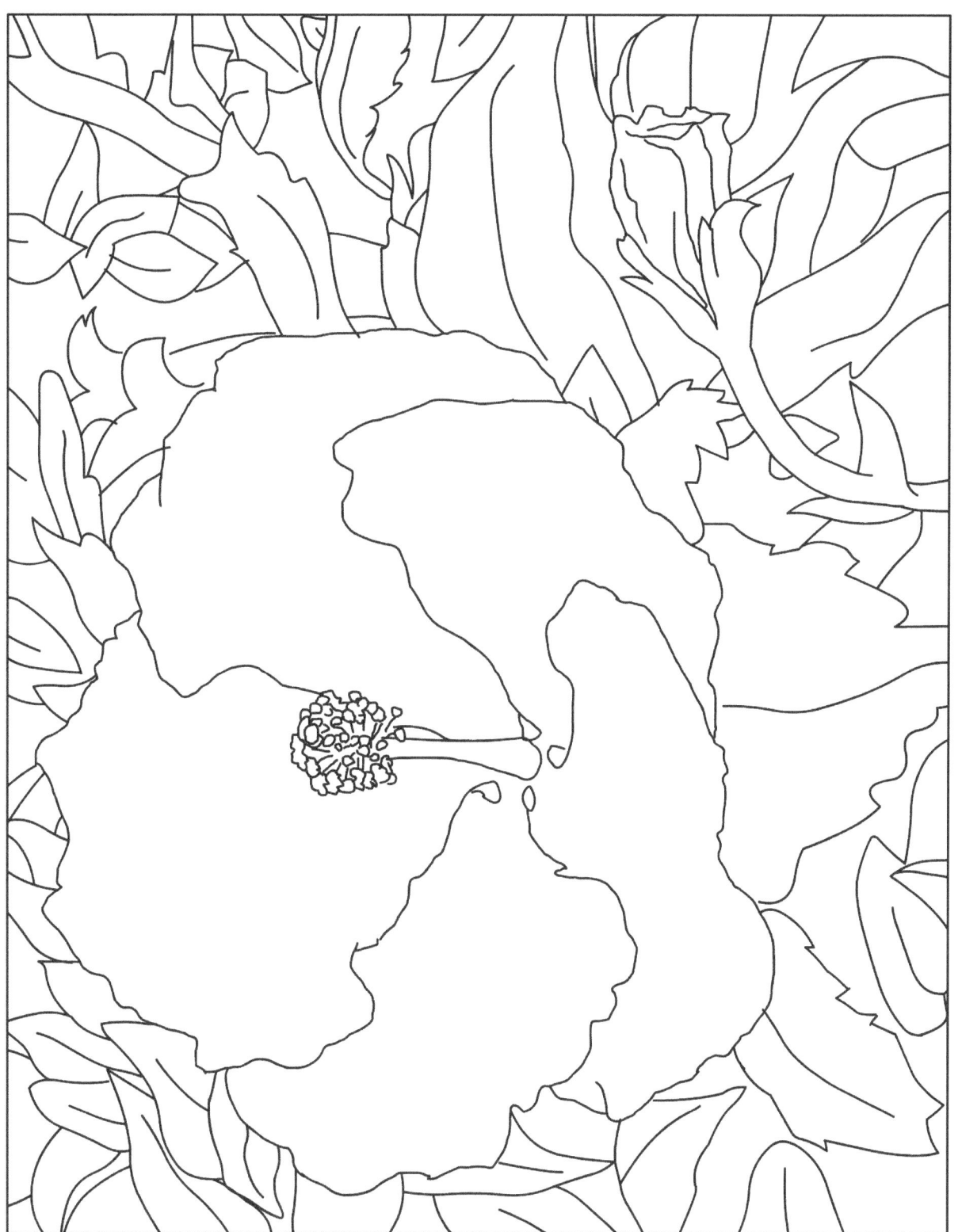

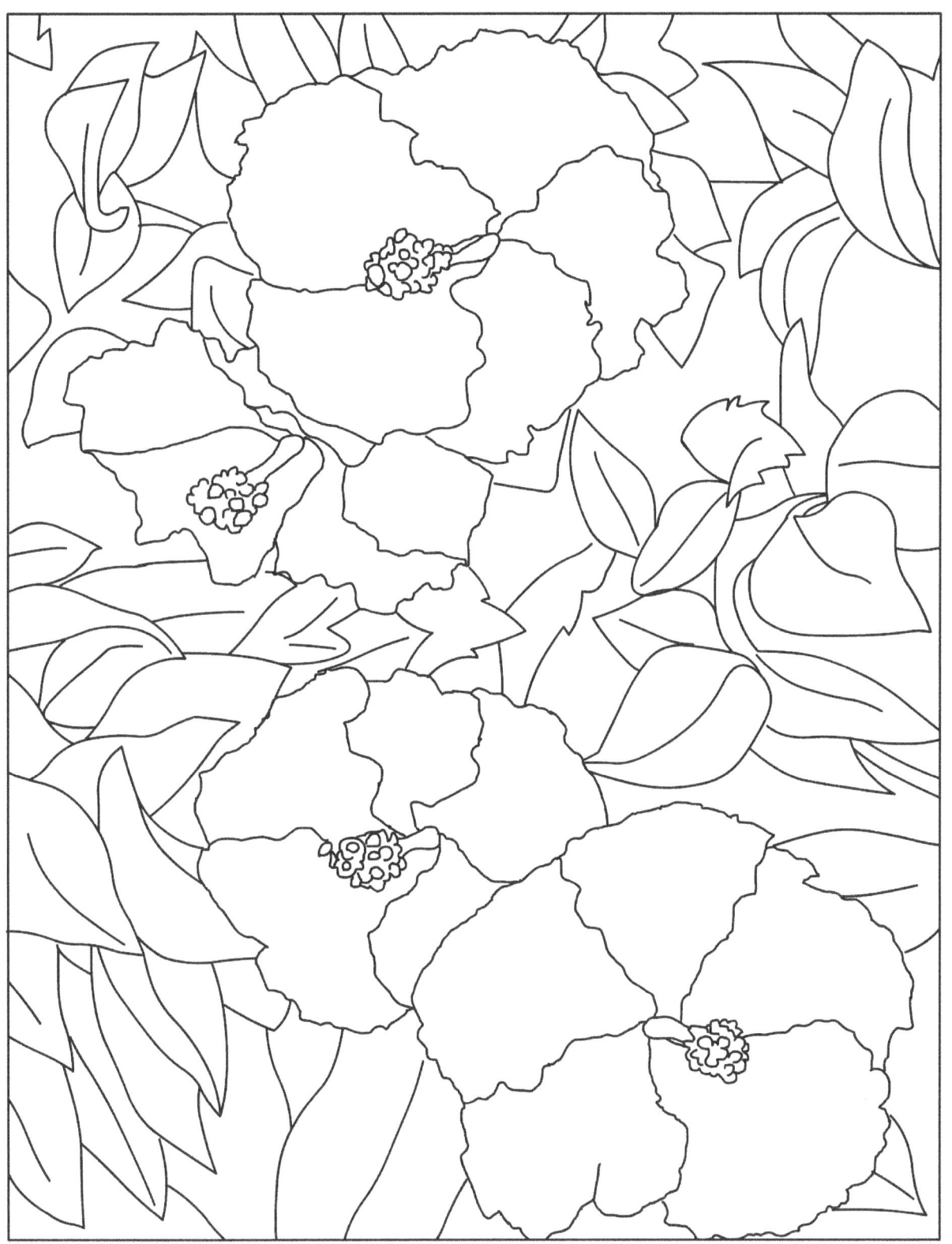

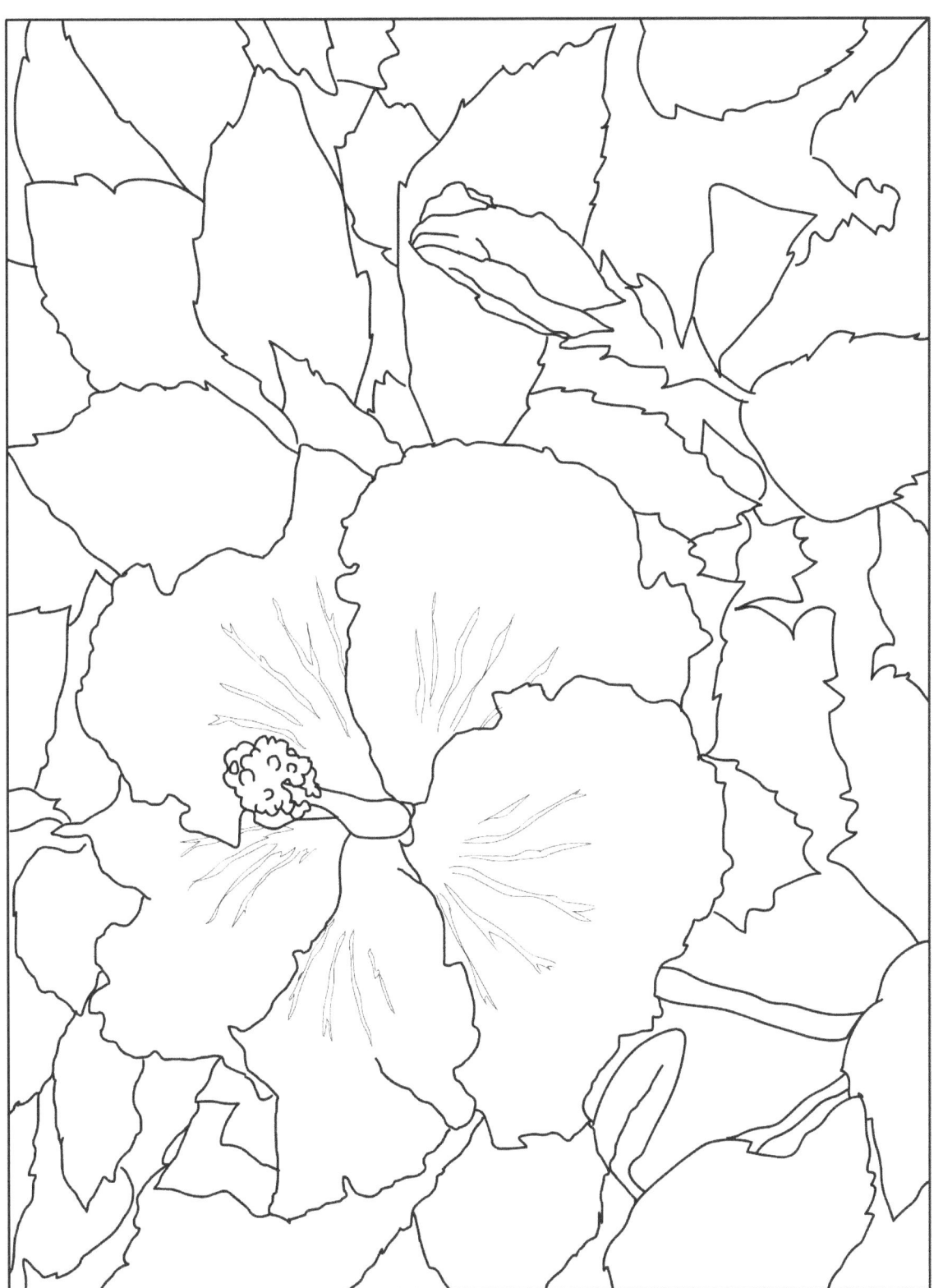

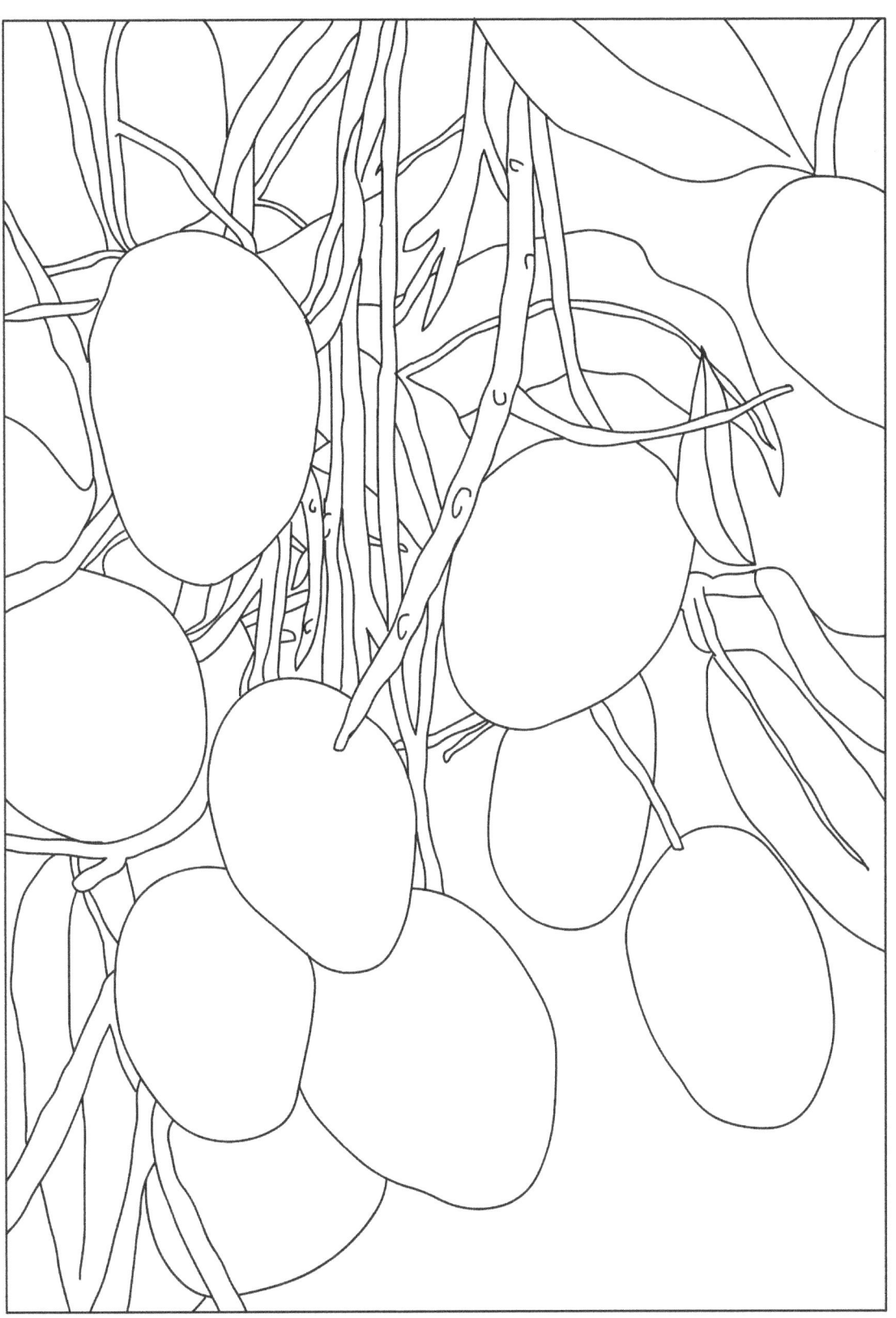

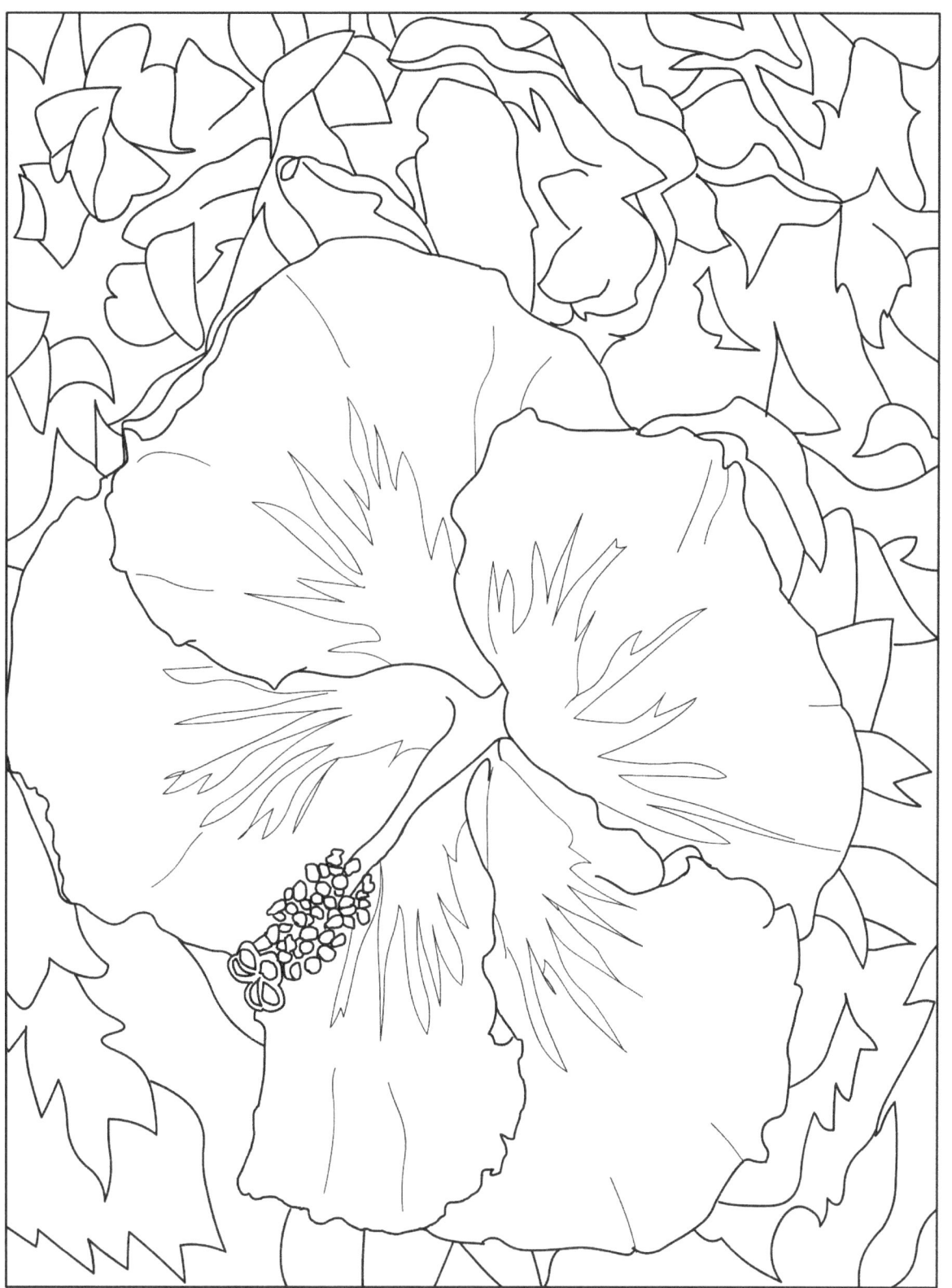

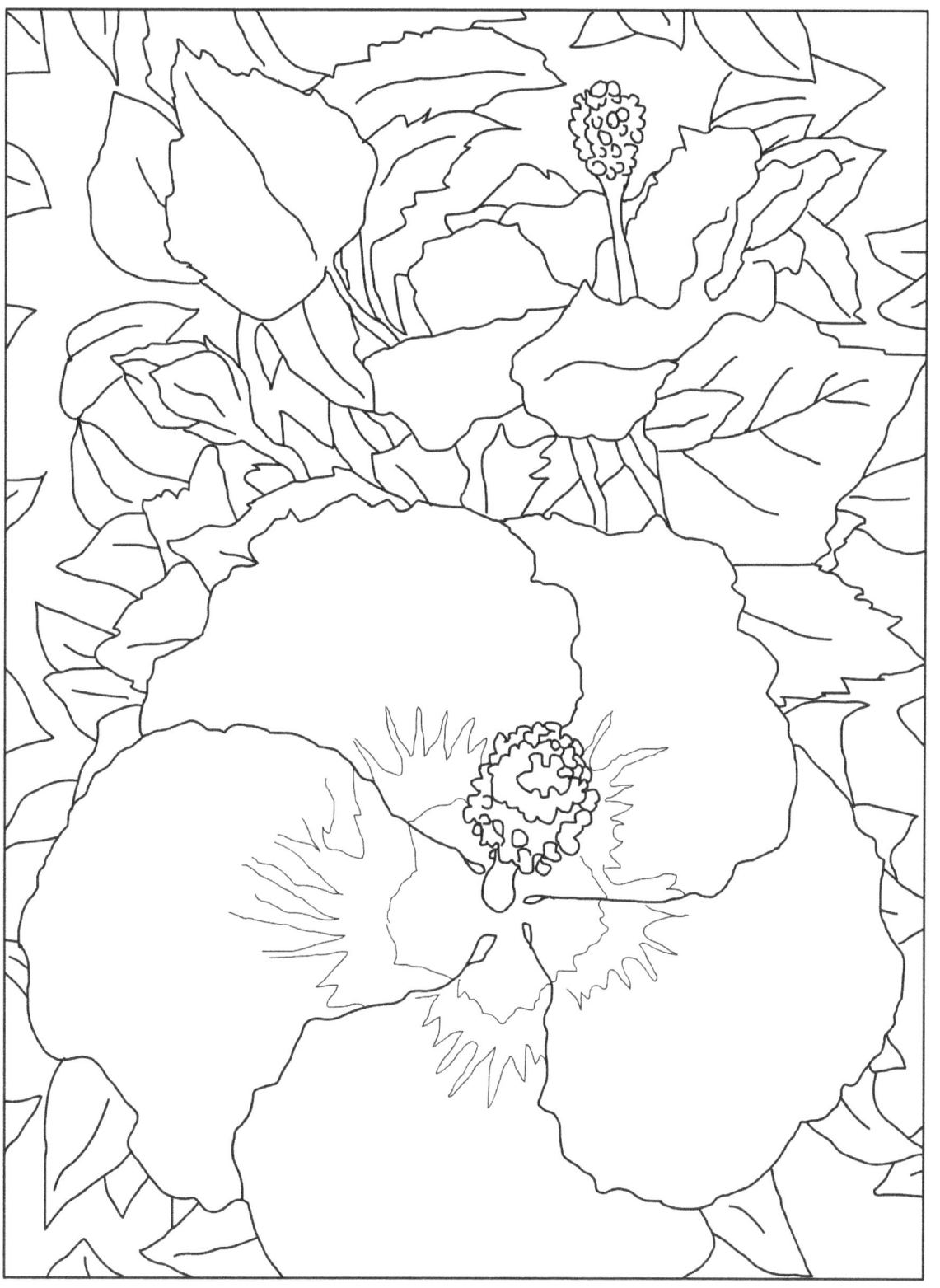

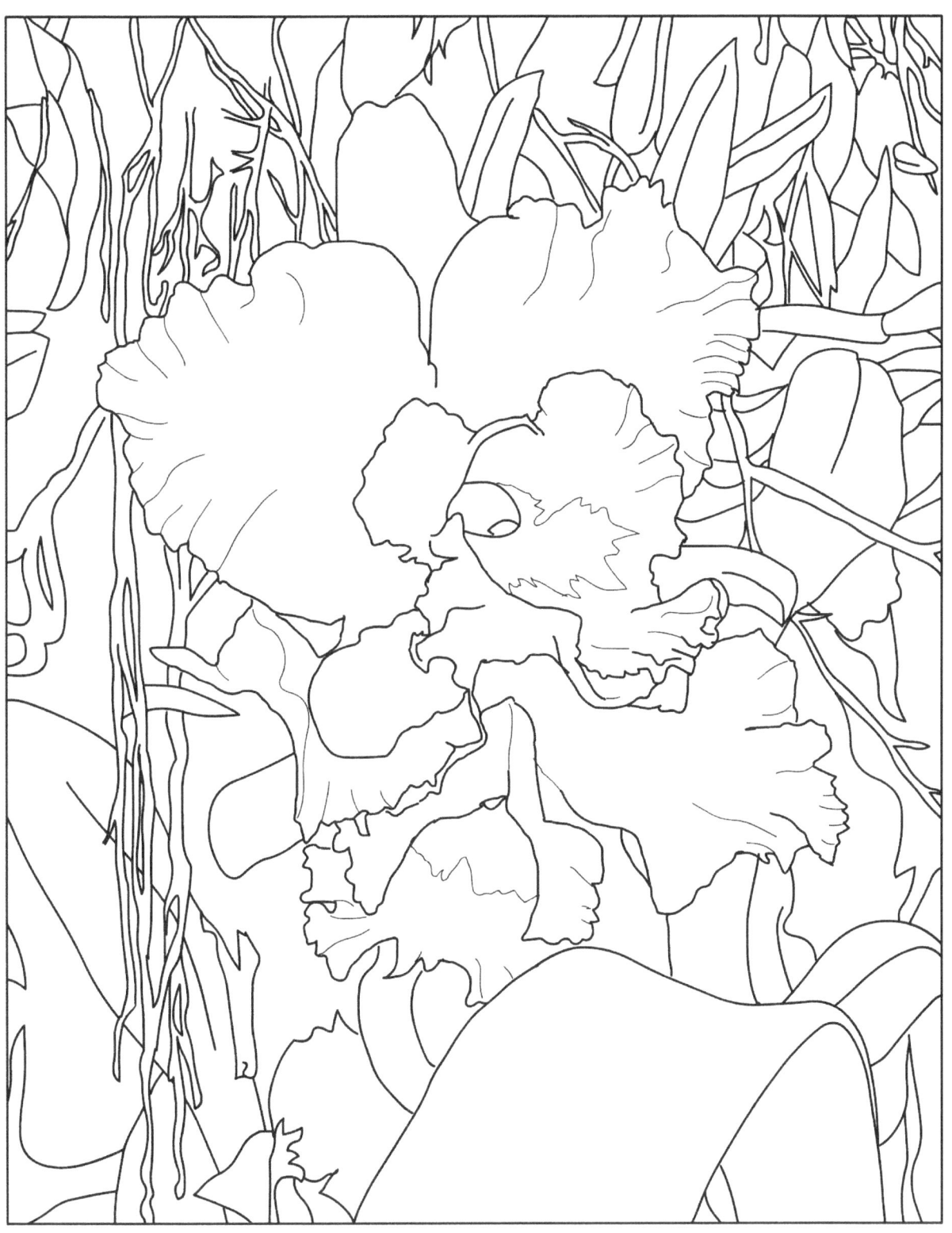

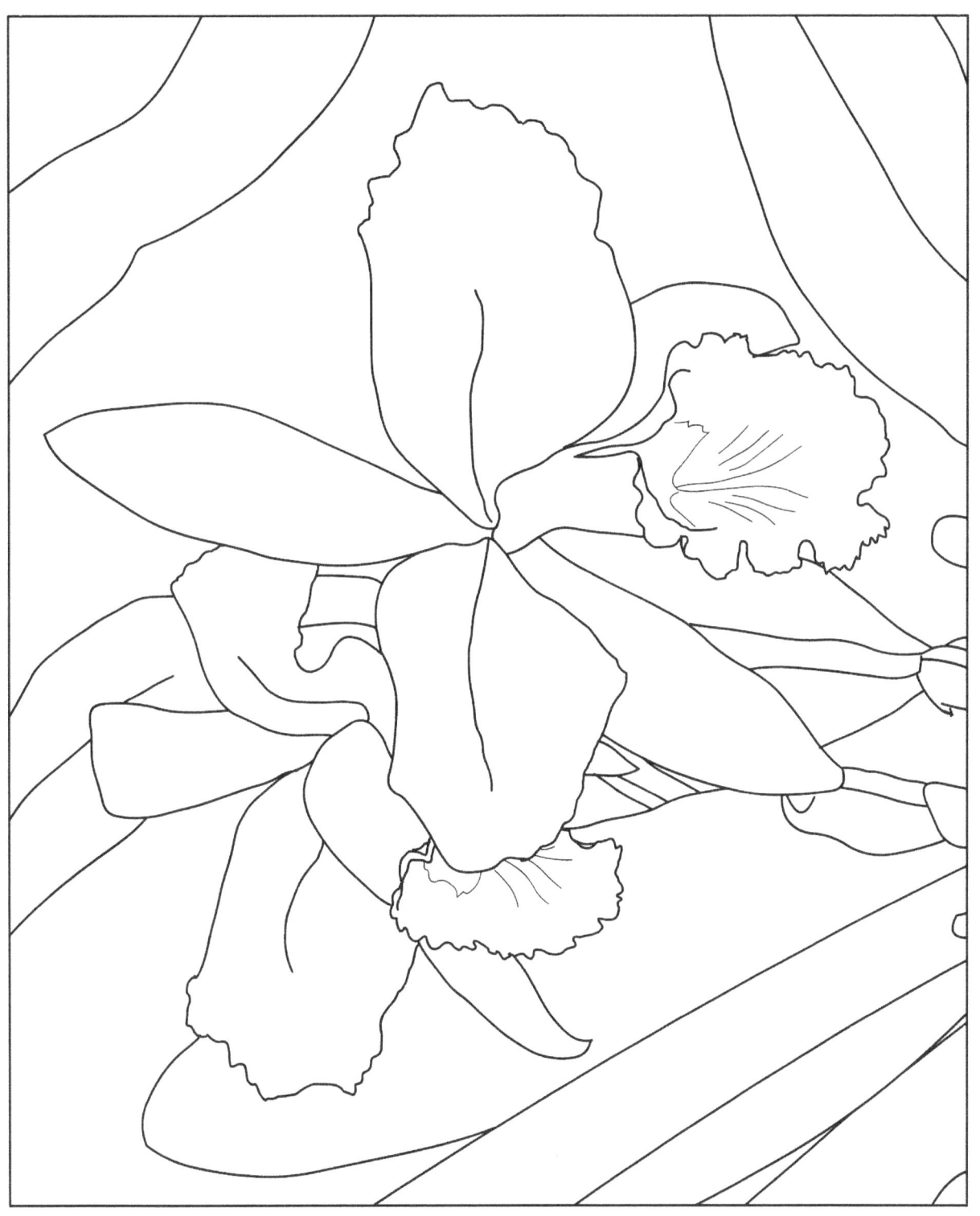

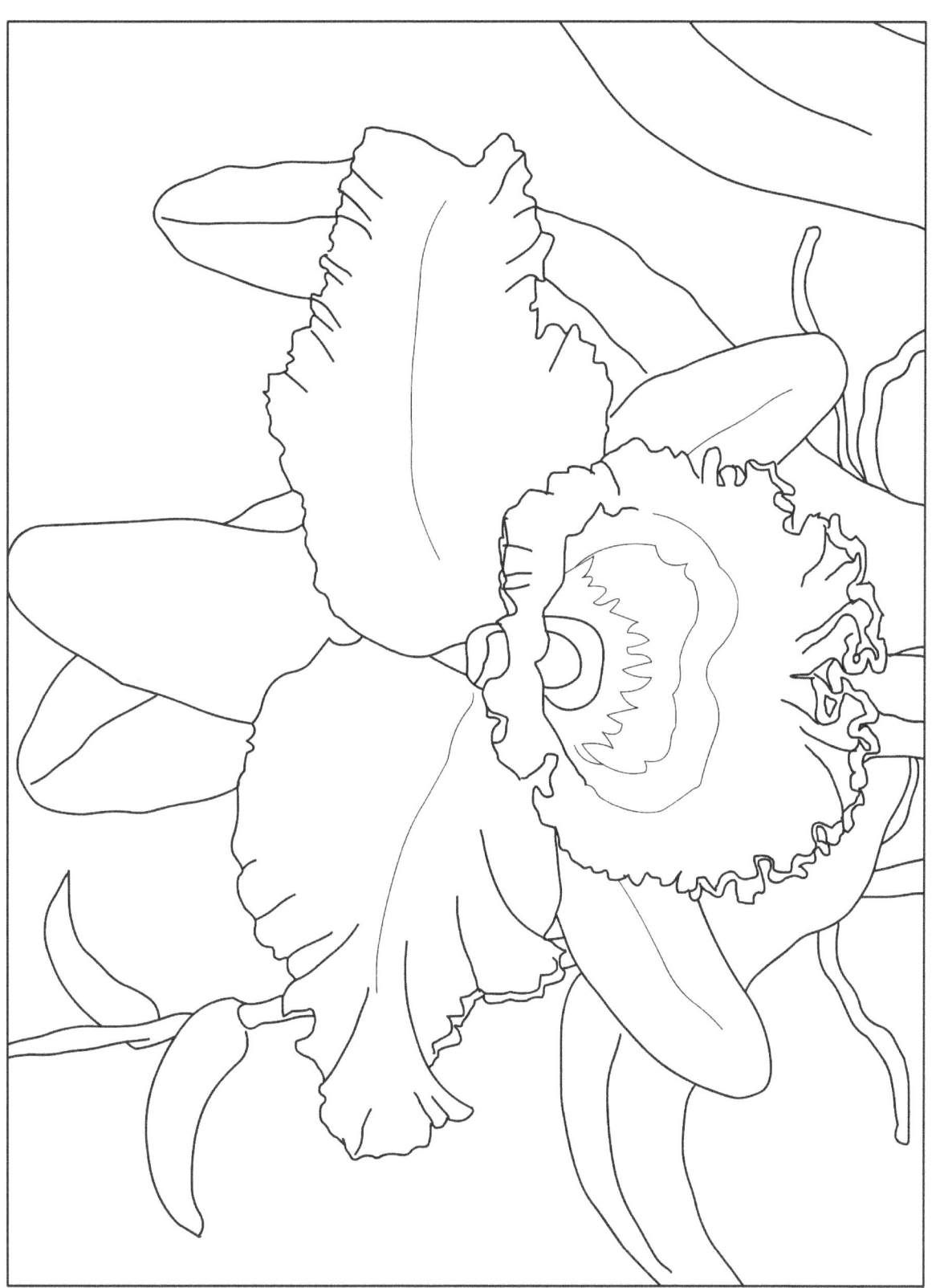

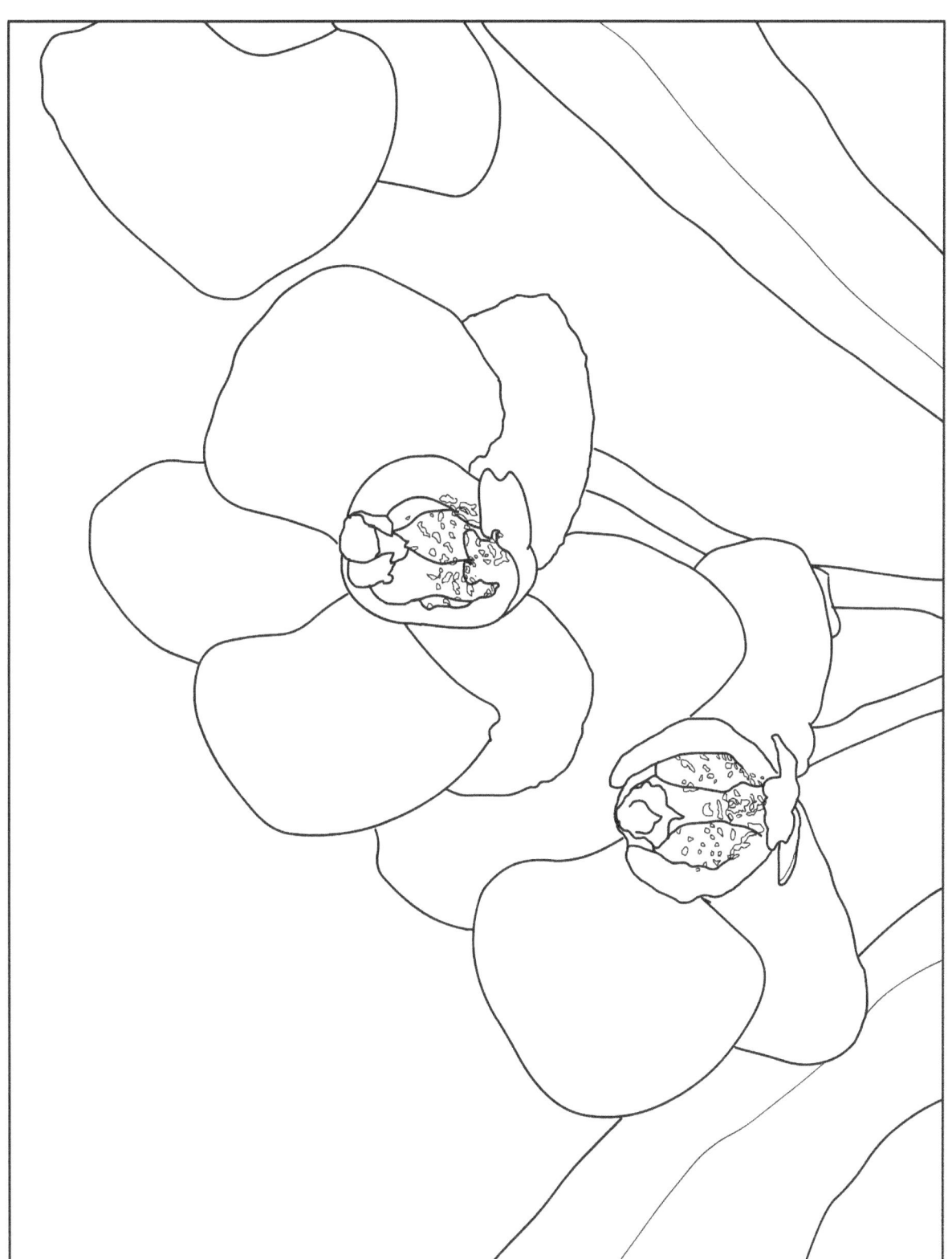

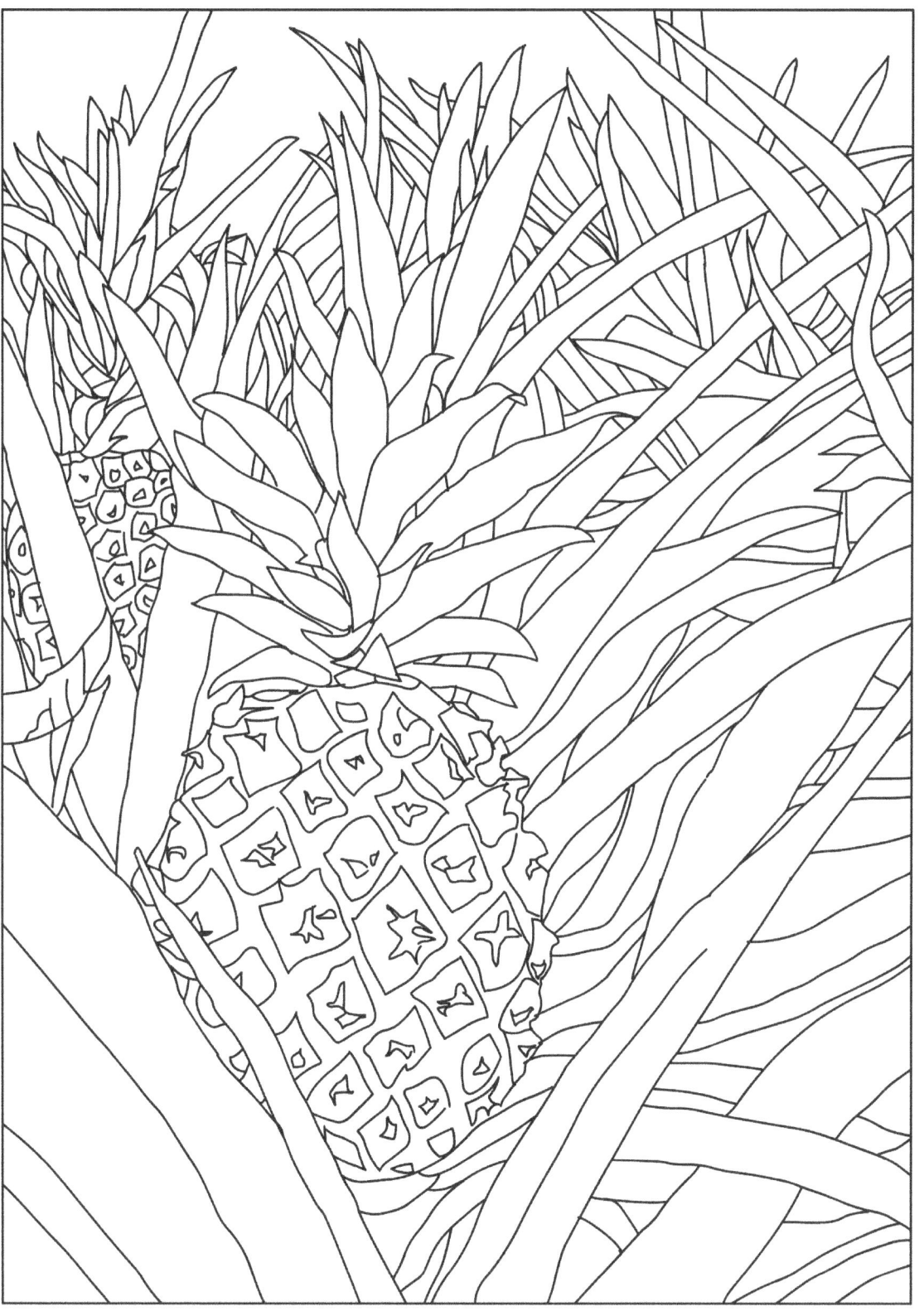

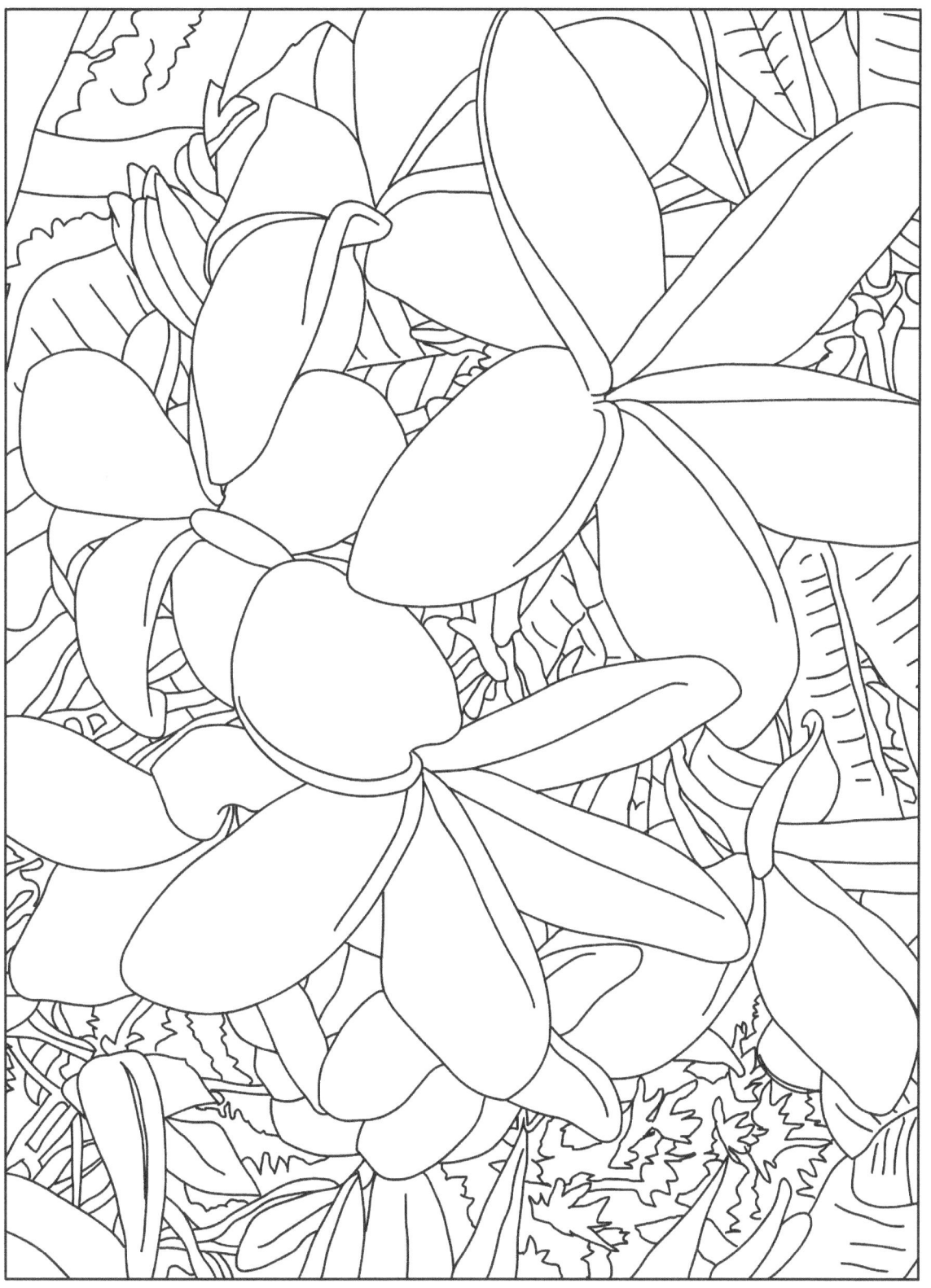

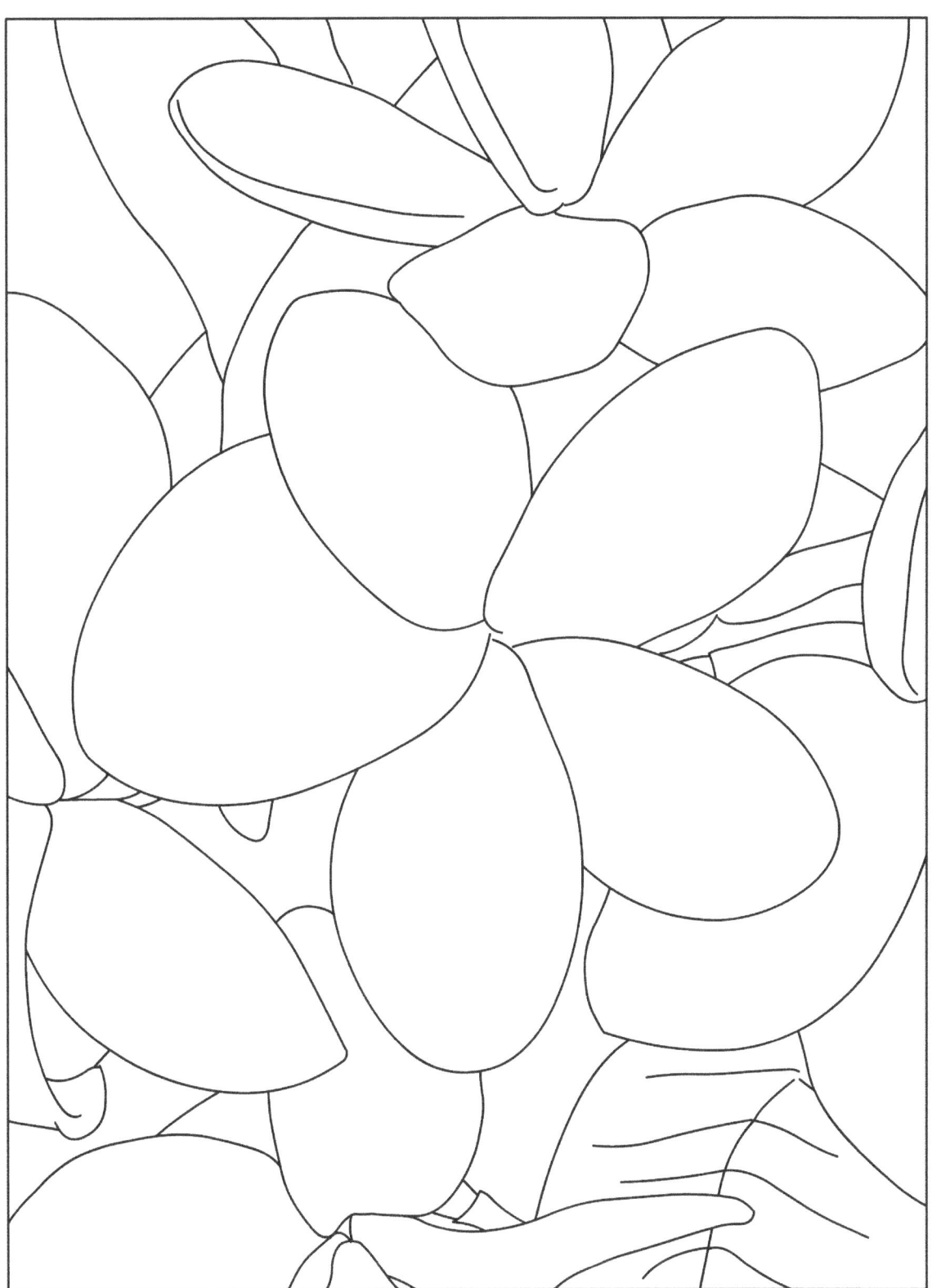

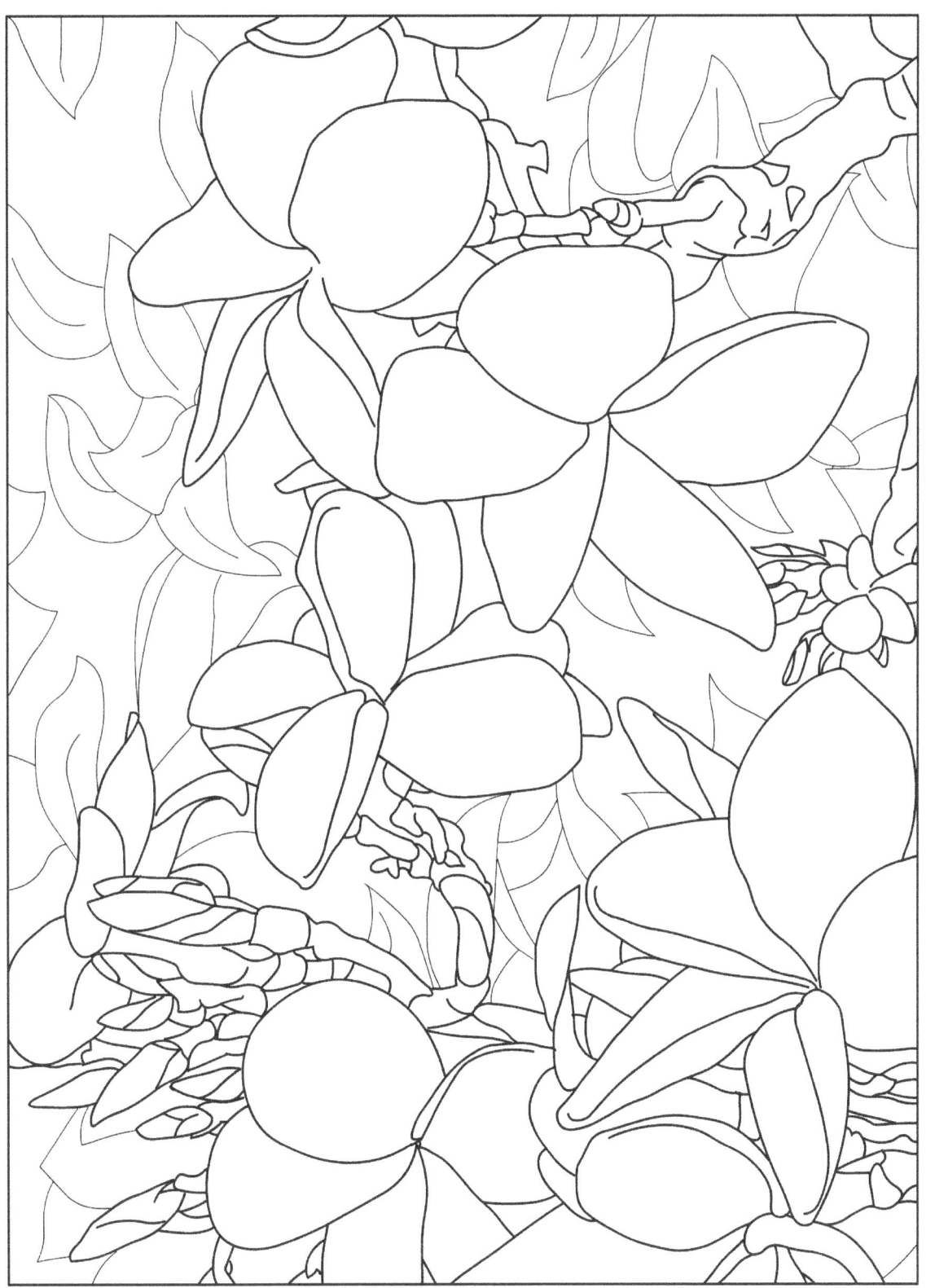

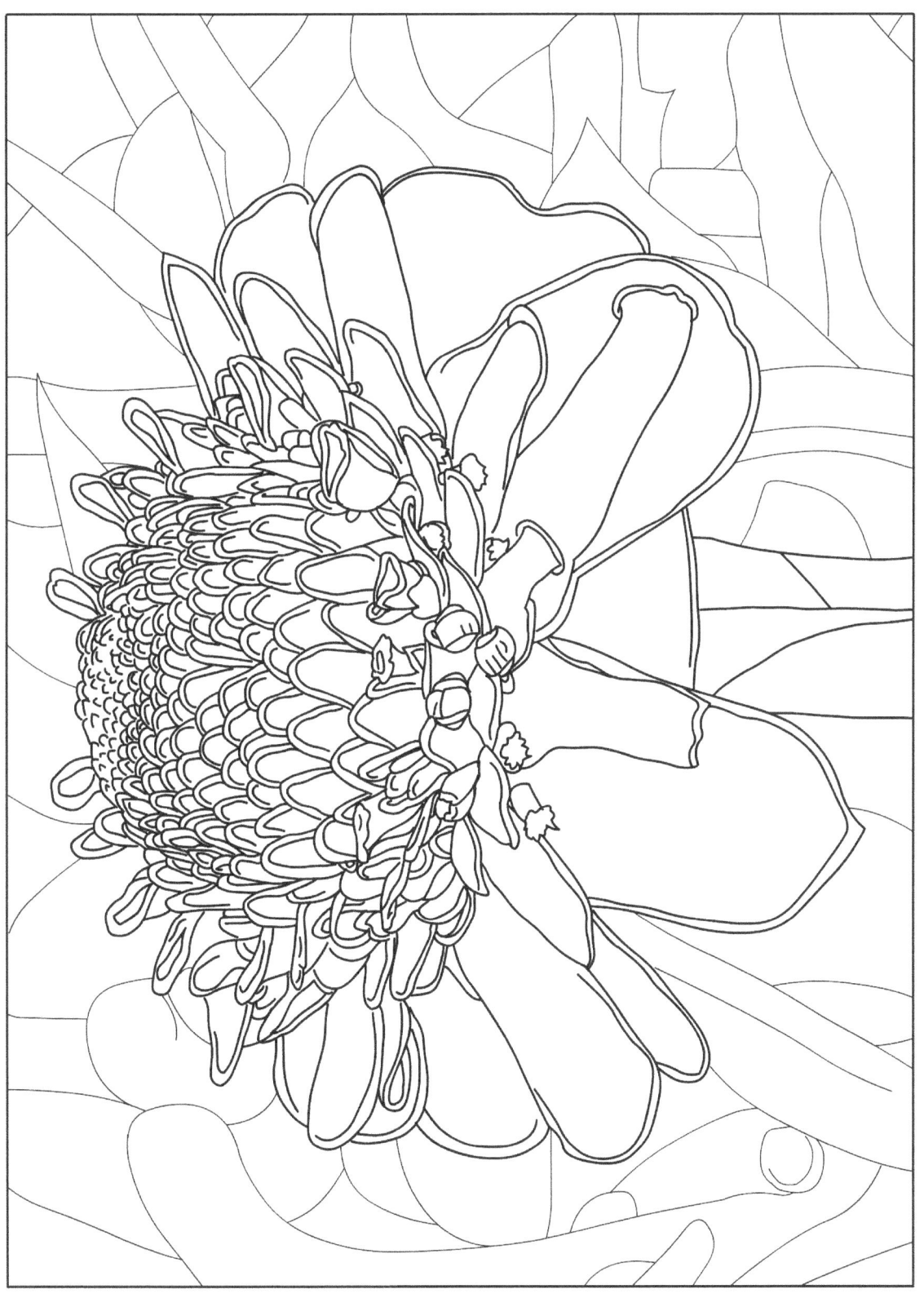

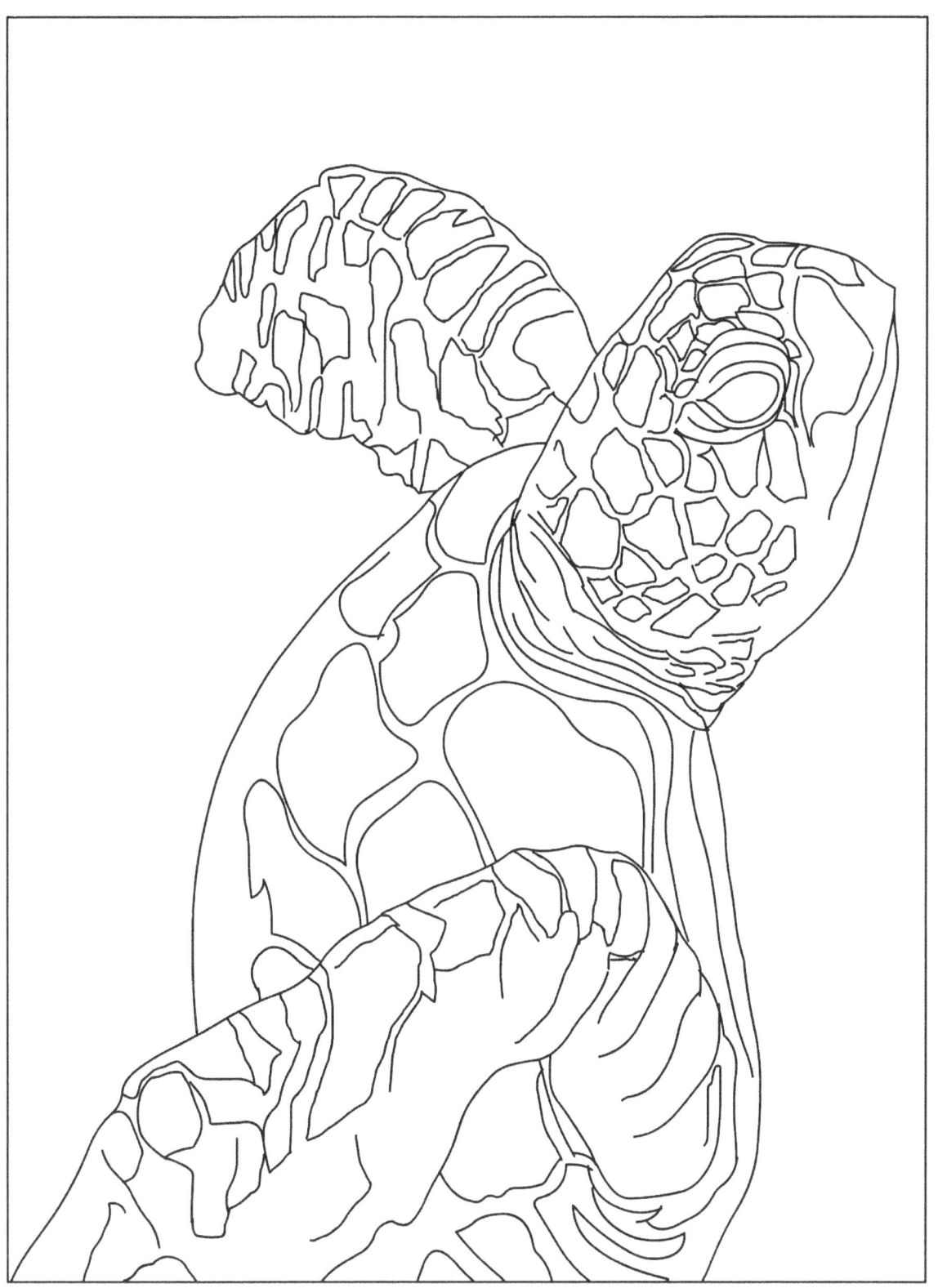

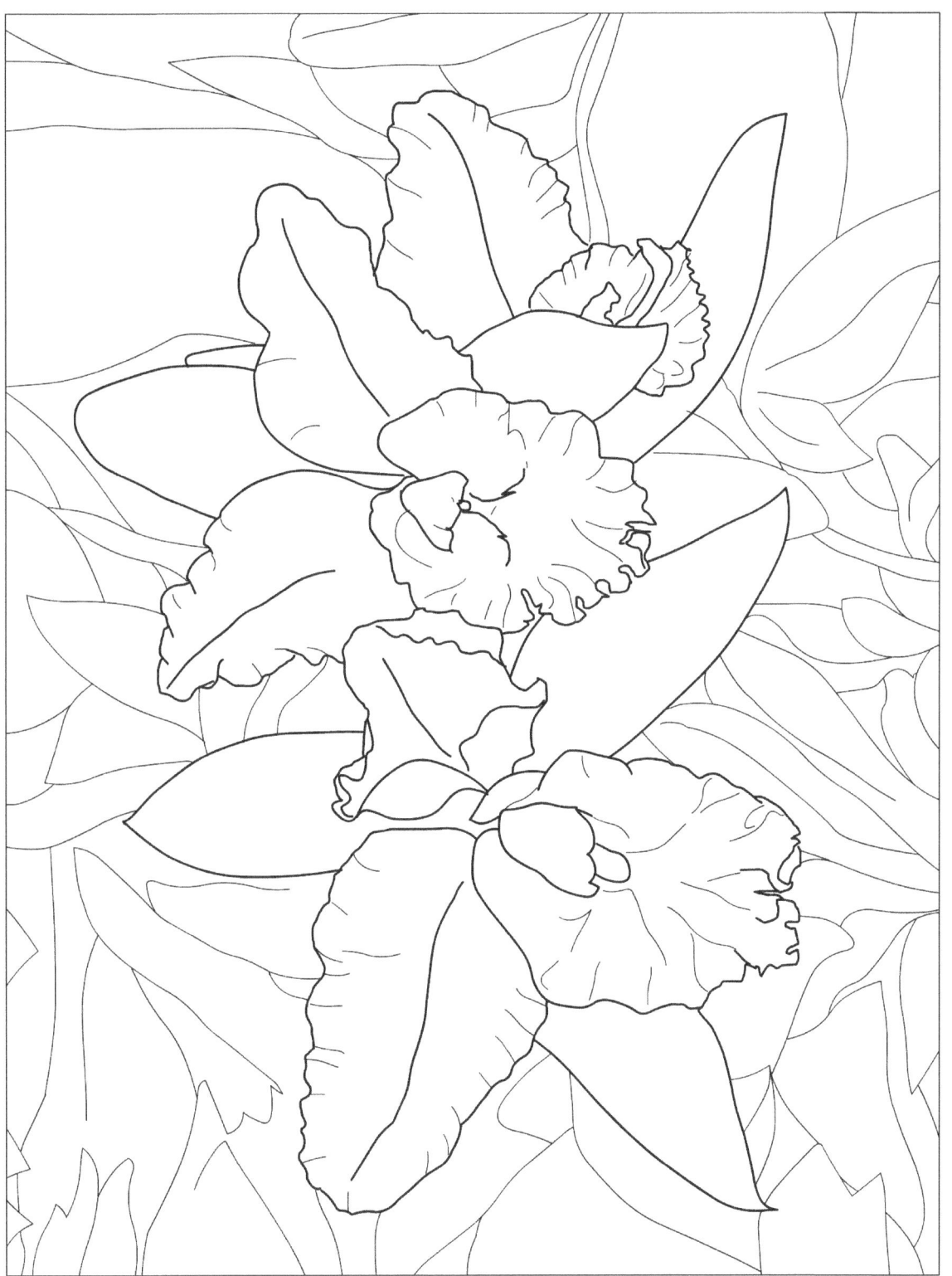

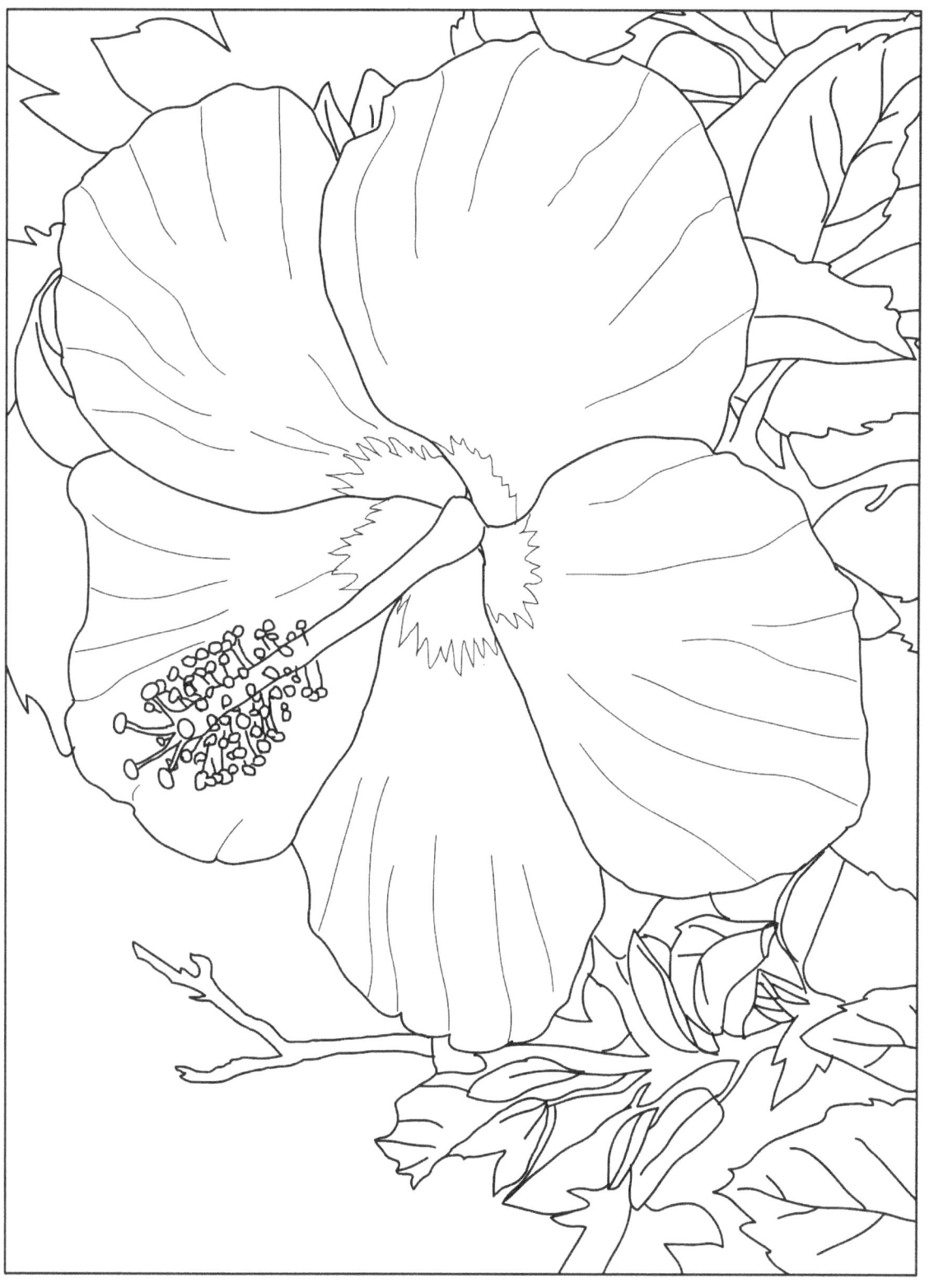

I have over a hundred large Hawaiian canvas prints and paintings, and nearly 200 smaller watercolor/prints at my Etsy art site. The coloring book pages are based on some of these. If you like my Hawaiian art, check these out at hawaiiseascapes.etsy.com

Check out my other books at Amazon. I have these books currently published:

Psychedelic Brain Freeze: An Adult Coloring Book. Psychedelic patterns for you to color.

Psychedelic Brain Freeze II: An Adult Coloring Book. More far out Psychedelic patterns.

 The Making of Psychedelic Brain Freeze: An Illustrated Book for Adults (explains the science behind optical illusions, shows how to color large poster sized pages to make your own art.)

The Making of Psychedelic Brain Freeze II: An Illustrated Book for Adults (explains the science for more optical illusions, shows how to color large poster sized pages to make your own wall art.)

 Relaxing Hawaiian Scenes, An Adult Coloring Book (first in the series)

 Relaxing Hawaiian Scenes II, An Adult Coloring Book (2nd in the series)

Portraits of President Donald Trump and the First Family: an Adult Coloring Book (attractive personal pictures of all of President Trump's family)

<u>Making of Portraits of President Donald Trump and the First Family, An Illustrated Book</u> (explains some of the hidden Easter egg images in the drawings)

 <u>How to Import From China Starting With $250 and Make a Small Fortune!</u>

 <u>Creation of the Universe and Other Strange Mormon Beliefs Revealed. (A church member tells all the Secrets the Authorities Don't Want to Talk About.)</u>

 <u>How To Use Your Money Making Genes to Become a Success and Make a Small Fortune.</u>

 <u>How to Publish Books on Amazon Kindle and Make a Small Fortune, The E-Book Money Making System</u>

Thanks....

.